Disney · PIXAR

Cars 2

THE ESSENTIAL GUIDE

Written by Steve Bynghall

CONTENTS

WGP

INTRODUCTION

LIFE IS GOOD FOR racing superstar Lightning McQueen. He has just won the Piston Cup for a fourth time and now he is heading back home to Radiator Springs for a well-earned rest. After an exhausting season burning rubber on the track, Lightning can't wait to hang out with Mater, Sally, and all of his friends.

However, instead of resting his tires in Radiator Springs, Lightning finds himself competing against the world's best race cars in the World Grand Prix. And it is all thanks to his best pal Mater! As Lightning travels from Tokyo to London, dreaming of winning the ultimate prize, all is not what it seems. It is up to Mater to save the day, but pretty soon, the rusty tow truck is caught up in an international spy adventure of his own...

RADIATOR SPRINGS

RADIATOR SPRINGS was founded in 1909 on the site of a natural spring, by a car named Stanley. This desert town is full of colorful characters and a steady stream of visitors, all curious to see where the famous Lightning McQueen lives. Radiator Springs is also one of the friendliest places on the planet!

DID YOU KNOW?

Radiator Springs is the gateway to Ornament Valley. Cars travel many miles just to see the breathtaking scenery here.

Lightning McQueen

Lightning is Radiator Spring's newest and most famous resident. He ended up here by accident, but found so many friends that he never left!

The Gang!

All the residents of Radiator Springs help make the town a fun and vibrant place to live. They always look out for each other, no matter what!

Fillmore

Love and peace, dude! Hippy Fillmore is the guy to see if you want tie-dyed mud flaps.

Sarge

Attention! Sarge is an ex-army Jeep, and applies his military mind to running an army surplus store.

Lizzie

Lizzie is the town's oldest resident. She might be forgetful, but she is youthful in outlook!

Ramone

Ramone runs his own paint shop, the House of Body Art, and regularly practices his skills on himself.

Flo

Flo is married to Ramone. She runs the V8 Café, where she serves the best (and only) fuel for miles around.

Red

Popular Red is the town fire truck. He is painfully shy and often emotional, especially about Radiator Springs.

Luigi

Italian Luigi runs the tire shop, Casa Della Tires with Guido. Luigi is completely obsessed with Ferraris!

Guido

Guido is an Italian forklift. Inseparable from Luigi, he works very hard at Casa Della Tires.

Sally

Sally is Lightning's girlfriend. She is the town's attorney and the owner of the Cozy Cone Motel.

Sheriff

Sheriff takes his job very seriously. He ensures that there is law and order in the town at all times.

Mater

Mater is the town's fun loving tow truck and the rustiest resident that Radiator Springs has ever seen!

WORLD GRAND PRIX

THREE DIFFERENT RACES, three different countries, one overall winner! Miles Axlerod, a former oil tycoon, has created the ultimate international racing challenge to debut his new alternative fuel, Allinol. The World Grand Prix is a once-in-a-lifetime gathering of the world's top race cars. This epic event will determine exactly who is the fastest car in the world!

Brent Mustangburger

Broadcaster Brent Mustangburger commentates on every race. Almost as famous as the cars themselves, he gives the must-have track analysis for TV viewers, along with Darrell Cartrip and David Hobbscap.

DID YOU KNOW?

Veteran TV commentators Darrell Cartrip and David Hobbscap also commentated on the Piston Cup.

The Racetracks

The WGP racecourse is like nothing ever seen before, with all three races set against a backdrop of breathtaking scenery.

RACE 1

Tokyo, Japan

The Tokyo race is a nighttime race that runs through the heart of the colorful city.

RACE 2

Porto Corsa, Italy

The Porto Corsa racetrack is set among views of the Italian Riviera and is a race fan favorite.

RACE 3

London, England

The finale in London takes the cars past iconic scenery, including Buckingham Palace.

And They're Off!

At the start of the Tokyo race, anticipation reaches fever pitch. With the crowd roaring, the race cars try hard to focus as the starting lights turn from red to green. Let the WGP begin!

The Race Cars

The international race cars come from different racing disciplines—LMP, Formula, GT, F6000 Cup Series, and Rally cars are all represented at the WGP.

Francesco Bernoulli (Formula)

Rip Clutchgoneski (F6000)

Jeff Gorvette (GT)

Shu Todoroki (LMP)

Max Schnell (WTC)

Miguel Camino (GT)

Carla Veloso (LMP)

Nigel Gearsley (GT)

Raoul ÇaRoule (Rally)

Lightning McQueen (Piston Cup)

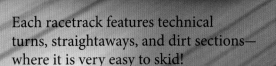

Lewis Hamilton (GT)

Each racetrack features technical turns, straightaways, and dirt sections—where it is very easy to skid!

MEET THE RACERS

THE WORLD GRAND PRIX has the greatest starting line up in history! As competitive as they are talented, the race cars are desperate to see the checkered flag and win the championship. On the racetrack, these guys are rough rivals, but off the track, they are good friends…at least most of the time!

LIGHTNING McQUEEN

COUNTRY:	USA
HOMETOWN:	Radiator Springs
TYPE:	Stock race car
TOP SPEED:	220 mph/354 km/h
HONORS:	Piston Cup
RACING STRENGTH:	Speed

The Favorite
With speed, stamina, and strength, Lightning is undoubtedly the best all-rounder on the track.

FRANCESCO BERNOULLI

COUNTRY:	Italy
HOMETOWN:	Monza
TYPE:	Formula
TOP SPEED:	185 mph/300 km/h
HONORS:	Formula Racer Champion
RACING STRENGTH:	Self-confidence

The Challenger
If anybody can beat Lightning, it's Francesco. He doesn't have a secret formula—just sheer talent!

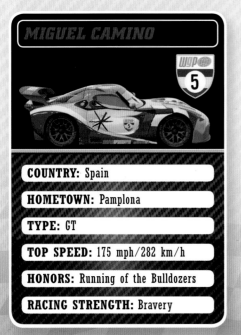

MIGUEL CAMINO

COUNTRY:	Spain
HOMETOWN:	Pamplona
TYPE:	GT
TOP SPEED:	175 mph/282 km/h
HONORS:	Running of the Bulldozers
RACING STRENGTH:	Bravery

The Fighter
Miguel is an expert bulldozer fighter! Funny and stylish, he loves to delight the crowd with his speed and flair.

LEWIS HAMILTON

COUNTRY:	UK
HOMETOWN:	Hertfordshire
TYPE:	GT
TOP SPEED:	165 mph/266 km/h
HONORS:	Junior, Formula Series
RACING STRENGTH:	Technical skill

The Contender
Smooth, sophisticated, and supremely confident, Lewis Hamilton has a habit of winning everything.

JEFF GORVETTE

COUNTRY:	USA
HOMETOWN:	Vallejo, CA
TYPE:	GT
TOP SPEED:	250 mph/400 km/h
HONORS:	Rookie of the Year
RACING STRENGTH:	Consistency

The Legend
Jeff Gorvette has the highest number of top 10 wins. He commands awe and respect on the racetrack.

CARLA VELOSO

WGP 8

COUNTRY: Brazil

HOMETOWN: Rio de Janeiro

TYPE: LMP

TOP SPEED: 175 mph/282 km/h

HONORS: Interlagos record holder

RACING STRENGTH: Rhythm

The Racing Queen
Carla loves to dance samba at the Brazilian car-nival, but she loves to win racing trophies even more!

NIGEL GEARSLEY

WGP 9

COUNTRY: UK

HOMETOWN: Warwickshire

TYPE: GT

TOP SPEED: 150 mph/241 km/h

HONORS: Grand Touring Champion

RACING STRENGTH: Stamina

The Expert
Cool car Gearsley learned to race by winning the Speed Hill Climb—an uphill race held in England.

SHU TODOROKI

WGP 7

COUNTRY: Japan

HOMETOWN: Mount Asama

TYPE: LMP

TOP SPEED: 250 mph/400 km/h

HONORS: Suzuka Champion

RACING STRENGTH: Determination

The Dragon
Shu is as competitive and fierce as the legendary red dragon Ka-Riu, which is part of his design!

MAX SCHNELL

WGP 4

COUNTRY: Germany

HOMETOWN: Stuttgart

TYPE: GTC

TOP SPEED: 180 mph/290 km/h

HONORS: Motorheimring Champion

RACING STRENGTH: Analytical mind

The Tactician
Max Schnell is a superb tactician. He studies the racetrack intensely before every race!

RAOUL ÇaROULE

WGP 6

COUNTRY: France

HOMETOWN: Alsace

TYPE: Rally

TOP SPEED: 200 mph/322 km/h

HONORS: French rally circuit

RACING STRENGTH: Flexibility

The Acrobat
Raoul used to be in the French circus. His natural gracefulness has helped him win many races!

RIP CLUTCHGONESKI

WGP 10

COUNTRY: Republic of New Rearendia

HOMETOWN: New Rearendia

TYPE: F6000 Cup Series

TOP SPEED: 240 mph/386 km/h

HONORS: None...yet

RACING STRENGTH: Enthusiasm

The Rookie
Rookie race car Rip has qualified in a number of races. He really could be the wildcard at the WGP.

LIGHTNING McQUEEN

RACING LEGEND LIGHTNING McQueen is the greatest athlete of his generation. Focused, fierce, and incredibly fast on the track, he has an awesome record of results. Despite being a highly successful, world-famous celebrity, Lightning's close friends in Radiator Springs ensure his wheels stay firmly on the ground.

DID YOU KNOW?
Lightning has won the prestigious Hudson Hornet Memorial Piston Cup once, and the Piston Cup a phenomenal four times.

Lightning always races in red. He has a special paint job just for the WGP!

Lightning has been using Lightyear tires for years

Best Friends

Lightning's unlikely best buddy is rusty tow truck Mater. When they are both in Radiator Springs, the duo are inseparable. However, when Lightning goes off to race, Mater usually stays at home...until the World Grand Prix.

A Car that Cares

Once Lightning had a fast life on and off the track, lapping up attention from his fans. But Lightning was unhappy and he realized that friends were more important than his career.

Brand new set of state-of-the-art headlights

STATS

Nationality	American
Honors	Piston Cup champion
Racing Discipline	Stock car
Top Speed	220 mph/354 km/h
Likely to say	"Ka-chow!"

Hall of Fame

Lightning McQueen is a champion race car. But he faces some tough competition at the WGP from the likes of fellow American, Jeff Gorvette. Up against the best of the best at the WGP, can Lightning maintain his championship record?

MATER

MATER IS A FUN-LOVING, fantastically friendly, and very loyal tow truck. Running Radiator Springs' only salvage center, Mater keeps the residents entertained with his happy attitude. Most of the time Mater might appear to be on another planet, but he is one of the best friends you could find on Earth!

Mater's left headlight has been missing for years!

STATS

Nationality American

Position Lightning's best friend and owner of Tow Mater Towing and Salvage

Racing Discipline Driving backward

Top Speed 75 mph/121 km/h

Likely to say "Tow Mater, at your service."

Traveling to the WGP is a new challenge for Mater. In Tokyo, he suddenly suffers an embarrassing oil leak and races to the restroom. Mater is confused by which restroom to use as he is completely out of his element!

Mechanical Mind

Mater might not have the sharpest mind in town, but he is a bright spark when it comes to old cars and spare parts—a talent that proves useful in Tokyo.

Friendship dents earned on various adventures with best pal Lightning

Mater is a bit of a motormouth. He loves to talk, but sometimes his words can get him into trouble!

Mater has Lightning's number 95 painted on him when he becomes part of Team Lightning McQueen

Good Company

Mater loves to have a laugh. Whether he is telling tall tales or going out tractor tipping, Mater's sheer energy and sense of fun are infectious. He always sees the good in every car—even when they are definitely very bad!

MATER'S MISHAP

MATER IS NOT the cleverest of tow trucks and he has suffered many mishaps in his lifetime. However, leaking oil at a sophisticated Tokyo party has to be his most embarrassing! It is a race to the restroom for Mater to stop his leak. But the rusty tow truck gets more than a clean grille at the Japanese restroom!

1. Desperate Mater

A mixed-up Mater makes it to the restrooms to stop his leak. He fails at the first hurdle, however, when he enters the ladies restroom by mistake!

2. Which Button?

When cars in Japan need to go to the restroom, they can choose to listen to music or even watch their favorite television program!

3. Crazy Cartoon

A colorful cartoon tries to make the complicated decision of which option to choose easier—but Mater picks something he is definitely not expecting!

4. Jet Set

Water jets shoot up from the floor underneath Mater. It tickles! When it happens a second time, it takes Mater by surprise and he lets out a scream!

5. Bubble Trouble

Pink is not Mater's favorite color! But pressing the wrong button in a Japanese restroom can bring surprising results. Covered in pink soapy suds, Mater is a bit less rusty and a whole lot cleaner!

TEAM LIGHTNING McQUEEN

A RACE CAR IS NOTHING without a trusty pit crew. When Lightning enters the World Grand Prix, the residents of Radiator Springs are eager to help their friend win. Team Lightning McQueen might not be the most experienced pit crew, but each member brings his own special talents to the racetrack.

What's up Doc?

Early in his career, Lightning was lucky enough to have his friend Doc Hudson as his road crew chief. Lightning not only learned tactics from the three-time Piston Cup winner, but also about the focus and drive needed to win a race.

All the crew have headsets to hear each other and to hear Lightning

Luigi

Luigi is the team's tire specialist. Back in Radiator Springs, Luigi is surrounded by tires running his own tire emporium, Casa Della Tires. He is ready to give his all for Team Lightning McQueen.

Fillmore

Hippy Fillmore is the crew's expert on earth-friendly, alternative fuels. He has even created his own organic variety.

CARBURETOR
51237
COUNTY

Mouthpiece allows each crew member to speak to Lightning while he is on the racetrack

Guido

Guido is the fastest forklift around! He is the team pitty who carries out a Pit Stop tire change in record speed!

DID YOU KNOW?

The Radiator Springs' gang were all part of Lightning's pit crew in the Piston Cup tiebreaker. Guido was the fastest in the stadium!

Sarge

Sarge brings his sense of duty and military discipline to Team Lightning McQueen—that is when he is not bickering with Fillmore!

Let's hope Mater doesn't need to tow Lightning off the racetrack!

Mater

Mater is responsible for directing Lightning during the races. What could possibly go wrong?

FRANCESCO BERNOULLI

FAST, FLASH, AND FULL of himself, Francesco Bernoulli is the most successful race car in Europe. The Italian Grand Prix champion loves to tease his rivals about how he will win every race. However, behind all the big-mouthed bravado, Francesco is really a good sport.

The second WGP race is held in Francesco's hometown of Porto Corsa in Italy. The dynamic Italian is desperate to impress his home crowd.

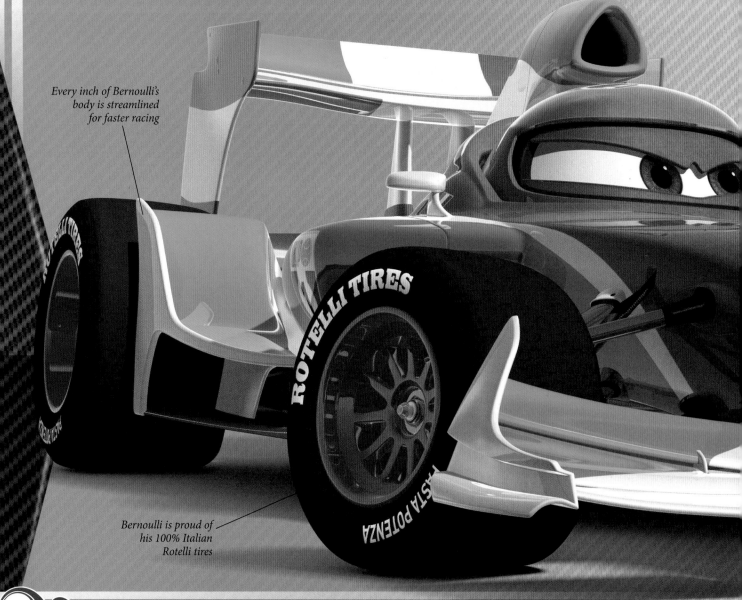

Every inch of Bernoulli's body is streamlined for faster racing

Bernoulli is proud of his 100% Italian Rotelli tires

ROTELLI TIRES

FASTA POTENZA

Numero Uno

Francesco passes his opponents on the racetrack through sheer power. But sometimes Bernoulli uses tactics and special track tricks to overtake his rivals. Whichever way, Francesco has the winning formula.

STATS

Nationality Italian
- -
Honors Formula Champion
- -
Racing Discipline Formula
- -
Top Speed 185 mph/300 km/h
- -
Likely to say "It is an honor... for you."
- -

Fantastic Fans

Francesco enjoys having a huge following of fans from around the world. They admire his sleek finish and open wheels. Even Lightning's girlfriend, Sally, admits the confident Italian is good-looking!

DID YOU KNOW?

When he was young, Francesco would sneak into the famous Monza race course and practice for hours.

Red, white, and green paint job—the colors of the Italian flag

RACING RIVALS

LIGHTNING McQUEEN and Francesco Bernoulli are the two greatest race cars on the planet, but there is only room for one champion! Pitched head-to-head in the WGP, their already intense rivalry just got serious. Although they won't admit it, deep down these two respect each other's amazing abilities on the racetrack.

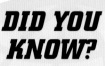

DID YOU KNOW?

Francesco is convinced he is going to beat Lightning, and has a bumper sticker on his rear that taunts him!

Tease Tactics

Francesco uses pre-race tactics to distract his rival. His specialty is to tease Lightning as much as possible. Francesco accuses Lightning of being scared of him, and only being able to drive around in circles!

"You are 'Speed?' Then Francesco is triple speed."

Bernoulli's tires have extra grip

Best of Three

With an audacious piece of skill, Francesco takes the checkered flag in Tokyo. However, Lightning soon gets things back on track with a win at Porto Corsa. With one race apiece, everything rests on the London race.
Will Lightning or Francesco be crowned WGP champion?

In addition to his brand new deco, Lightning gets a WGP decal

Cool Customer

Initially, Lightning is taken aback by the Italian's taunts! But before the big race in Tokyo, he remains focused by refusing to be annoyed by Francesco's words.

"Speed. I am speed."

UNCLE TOPOLINO

WARM, WELCOMING, and full of wise words, Uncle Topolino is Luigi's favorite uncle. He lives in the beautiful village of Santa Ruotina, just outside Porto Corsa, Italy. Uncle Topolino proves that Italian hospitality can't be topped when he invites Lightning's entire pit crew to stay.

Uncle Topolino is proud that his soft top is still in great condition!

Home Sweet Home

Luigi and Guido will always be grateful to Uncle Topolino—he turned them into tire experts! Years ago, they worked in his village tire shop, Topolino's. He inspired them to open their own tire shop, Casa Della Tires in Radiator Springs.

DID YOU KNOW?

Uncle Topolino is a 1937 Fiat model, but he is still in tip-top condition!

Mama Topolino

Luigi's aunt, Mama Topolino, produces the finest fuel in Santa Ruotina. She has made it her mission to make sure everyone in the village is well fed. The villagers always leave Mama's house with a full tank!

Wise Uncle

Uncle Topolino has years of experience under his hood—he is one of the oldest cars in Santa Ruotina! He is known as the wisest car in Italy. Cars near and far visit Uncle Topolino to ask his advice on everything, from tires to friendship.

MILES AXLEROD

MILES AXLEROD is a filthy rich oil tycoon. However, he has decided to clean up his act and use his energy and powers for the common good. Converting to an electric car and taking up the environmental cause, some find Miles' sudden conversion to campaigner almost too good to be true...

Solar panel

STATS

Nationality	British
Position	Founder of Allinol
Discipline	WGP creator
Top Speed	100 mph/161 km/h
Likely to say	"Alternative energy is the future!"

REGEN R8

Electric Dreams

Axlerod used to be a gas guzzler, but he is so devoted to making alternative energy the future, he has converted to electric. Miles is now very eco-conscious and even has a solar panel on his roof.

Wire coils in wheels are connected to electric battery

Green Miles

Miles is on the mission of a lifetime. The former oil baron is on a quest to find an alternative fuel. He may just have found it with Allinol, a clean-burning, renewable fuel. All in all, Axlerod has the determination, drive, and vision to see his wonder fuel succeed.

Miles knows good advertising. The Allinol logo is everywhere, even on his grille and tire treads!

Power Fuel

Miles has spent years developing his new fuel, Allinol. He has created the World Grand Prix to demonstrate the power of Allinol—the cleanest, safest, cheapest alternative fuel ever made. The planet's athletic elite will all be using it, proving it truly is an eco-friendly wonder fuel.

Axlerod's paint job is green to match his views

DID YOU KNOW?

Axlerod met the Queen of England when he was knighted and is actually "Sir" Miles Axlerod.

PROFESSOR Z

PROFESSOR Z is a mad scientist with a truly twisted mind. He spends his life in his laboratory, thinking up all manner of strange inventions. The unhinged genius's latest venture is a plot so extreme in its off-the-scale awfulness that he must be stopped at all costs!

The evil Professor has a secret hideout—a remote oil rig in the middle of the Pacific Ocean. Here, with the help of his minions, he is plotting to disrupt the WGP.

CLASSIFIED INFORMATION

Nationality German
Agency His own evil empire
Department Weapons Design
Top Speed 60 mph/97 km/h
Likely to say "Now no one can stop us!"

Mastermind

Professor Z has a brilliantly inventive brain. He has designed all sorts of weird and not-so-wonderful devices. His latest design is a dangerous weapon that will change the world forever. It is a tragedy the eccentric scientist's genius is used for such despicable ends!

The Professor's battered body is about to fall to bits

The Inventor's Henchcars

Professor Z relies on an army of unquestioning loyal Lemons—cars that are always breaking down—to carry out his cowardly plans. Acer and Grem act as the scientist's sidekicks, carrying out his dastardly deeds.

A monocle is the trademark of evil geniuses everywhere. It also helps the Professor look clever.

Z 750

Professor Z spends so much time in his lab, he doesn't have time to give his hubcaps a coating of Rust-eze!

EVIL INVENTION

PROFESSOR Z is involved in an appalling plot to discredit the alternative fuel, Allinol. He has invented a deadly electromagnetic radiation ray (disguised as a camera) to ruin the World Grand Prix. This might just be the Professor's most brilliant invention yet!

The lens viewer has a special light to help pinpoint the target

WANTED

INTERNATIONAL TRAFFIC AGENCY

1.5 m
1 m
.5

PROFESSOR Z

WEAPONS DESIGNER

Wanted!

Every country's secret service is hunting down Professor Z. His warped intention to invent the wickedest weapons means he is a threat to every single car on the planet.

The tripod is part of the disguise, but also keeps the weapon steady for any nervous Lemons!

Special Delivery

In the dead of night, a prototype of the weapon is delivered to Professor Z's oil derrick hideout. But the Lemons are being watched by top secret agent Finn McMissile, who secretly takes pictures of the strange device.

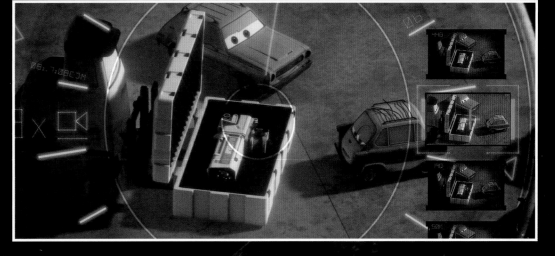

Smile for the Camera!

The weapon emits invisible blasts of electromagnetic radiation. If this is pointed toward a car filled with Allinol, the fuel starts to boil and expand. This forces the engine to crack and leak oil into the combustion chamber, which means the car may explode!

GREM AND ACER

ANGRY AUTOMOBILES Grem and Acer are Professor Z's chief henchcars. The dishonest duo are both Lemons—a global gang of cars who have design faults and performance problems. The Lemons have grown bitter about their situation and turn their trunks on society. They team up with the Professor in his evil scheme to become the most powerful cars in the world.

Lemons like Grem are envious of other cars, especially polished, sleek ones like secret agent Rod "Torque" Redline.

Grem

Grem is a Lemon who has a real zest for crime. The only good thing that can be said about Grem is that he enjoys his work!

STATS

Nationality	American
Family	Gremlin
Position	Professor Z's muscle
Top Speed	150 mph/242 km/h
Likey to say	"Smile for the camera!"

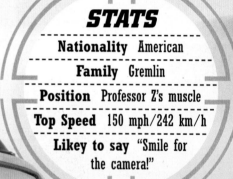

Dirty Grem could use a new paint job

Acer's windows could use a serious wash

STATS

Nationality	American
Family	Pacer
Position	Professor Z's muscle
Top Speed	150 mph/242 km/h

Likely to say
"He's getting away!"

Acer hopes to get a replacement bumper before this one falls off

Acer

Acer the Pacer has always felt like an outcast in the car world due to his beat-up appearance. He is as rough as he looks and doesn't care what harm he causes to other cars!

Victor H

The Lemon families are controlled by powerful Lemonheads. Victor H is head of the Hugo Lemon family. Victor is a very rich villain, making huge amounts of money running a network of corrupt oil refineries.

Acer isn't afraid to get his wheels dirty, doing the Professor's every bidding. However, Acer is no match for super-slick secret agent Finn McMissile.

FINN McMISSILE

FINN McMISSILE is a master secret agent from British Intelligence. Despite facing near-impossible dangers, unflappable Finn always completes his mission. Using all his cunning and charisma, Finn can maneuver out of the tightest corners and the stickiest situations!

Finn has concealed rocket launchers in his headlights. When he shoots his rockets they are always on target.

Bulletproof bodywork to protect Finn from his enemies

Finn's tires have special hidden protective armor

Secret Stockpile

Finn McMissile has a cool collection of weapons and gadgets to help him on every mission. One of his gadgets can even cut through glass! Of course, they are all hidden from view to make sure enemy agents are taken by surprise!

Sophisticated Finn

With many years of international espionage experience under his hood, Finn is the ultimate secret agent. He oozes "old school" British charm and is also highly intelligent—both essential when you work for British Intelligence!

Headlights conceal rocket launchers

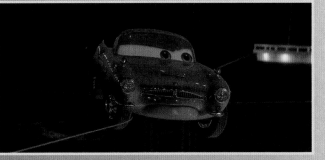

CLASSIFIED INFORMATION

Nationality British
Agency HM Secret Service
Department Field Agents
Top Speed 180 mph/290 km/h
Likely to say "Thanks, old boy!"

Often Finn has to work undercover in the darkness of night. He is an expert at hiding in the shadows, so his movements remain secret.

DID YOU KNOW?

Finn McMissile can turn himself into a submarine, so he can be undercover underwater!

HOLLEY SHIFTWELL

BRAVE BRITISH AGENT Holley Shiftwell is fresh out of the secret agent academy. Trained in all the latest techniques, Holley is the agent in the know if you need the lowdown on the latest state-of-the-art equipment. However, Holley is no gadget geek—she is a highly intelligent secret agent determined to succeed!

CLASSIFIED INFORMATION

Nationality British
Agency HM Secret Service
Department Tokyo Station
Top Speed 150 mph/242 km/h
Likely to say "This area may be compromised!"

Secret electroshockers that can fire blasts of electricity

Classy sports car

Holley is in Tokyo to deliver top secret information to Finn McMissile. She is a long way from home, but enjoys the challenge of being stationed in Japan.

Face your Fears

When she is unexpectedly thrust into the frontline on a top secret mission, Holley is nervous about working in the field for the first time. But she soon shifts up a gear, and draws on her well of talent to face new dangers!

Concealed tracking computer to locate almost anything

The Rookie Road

Mixing with a top secret agent like Finn McMissile puts the pressure on Holley. She might be a rookie agent, but Holley is willing to work hard to impress the experienced Finn with her enthusiasm.

DID YOU KNOW?

Holley has a pair of retractable wings hidden in her side that allow her to fly!

Holley has a stash of hidden gadgets to surprise her enemies!

SIDDELEY THE JET

BRITISH SECRET SERVICE jet plane Siddeley is exactly the sort of agent you want on your team. Ultra-reliable and brave, Siddeley will come to your rescue at just the right time. Many agents have breathed a sigh of relief as they have glimpsed silver-bodied Siddeley swooping down from the sky in order to lift them to safety.

Siddeley rescues Finn McMissile and Mater from the Lemons and then flies them and Holley Shiftwell all the way from Tokyo to Paris.

DID YOU KNOW?

One of Sid's close secret service pals is Stephenson, a spy train that takes Finn, Holley, and Mater from Paris to Italy.

Air Acrobatics

Siddeley is an extremely stylish jet. His luxurious interior is big enough to accomodate many secret agents embarking on top secret missions around the world.

Siddeley believes you do a better job when you are wearing a smile

Siddeley's sleek body is aerodynamically designed to reach super-fast speeds

CLASSIFIED INFORMATION

Nationality British
Agency HM Secret Service
Department Air Corps
Top Speed 350 mph/563 km/h
Likely to say: "I'm on approach!"

Twin jet engines with remarkable power for ultimate performance

Frequent Fliers

Siddeley and Finn McMissile have completed hundreds of successful missions together. Although Finn is a higher-ranking agent, he can always rely on Siddeley to fly to his rescue.

SUPER SPY GEAR

IS IT A BOAT? Is it a plane? No, it's a super secret agent! British secret agents Finn McMissile and Holley Shiftwell have been issued with an arsenal of the latest gear and gadgets to help them on their missions. Fooling the enemy is easy when you can change into a completely different form of transport. Watch out evil villains!

Rockets launch at super-speed causing huge explosions

Submarine Mode

Turning into a submarine is sometimes the only way to escape dangerous situations. Enemies will think you have perished in the sea, when in fact you are swimming deep under the water.

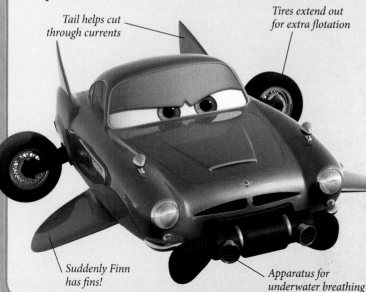

Tail helps cut through currents

Tires extend out for extra flotation

Suddenly Finn has fins!

Apparatus for underwater breathing

Agent McMissile

Finn has been a secret agent for many years and remembers when the gadgets were not so good. These days, everything is so advanced—he is always amazed by the latest clever inventions!

DID YOU KNOW?

Finn and Holley are equipped with a powerful computer that has a databank of information about enemies and where they might be.

Guns on both sides for extra fire-power

Hydrofoil Function

Turning yourself into a boat will certainly foil your enemy! They will be taken by surprise when you make a speedy getaway across the surface of the water.

Special skis skim water

Finn is a hot-shot and a sharp shooter!

Airplane Mode

If you are ever blocked in a corner by villains, just operate airplane mode. One of the most amazing pieces of spy gear, airplane mode allows agents to fly through the air. But it's not just for high fliers—it is standard issue for all new agents.

Rear tail extends upward to help smooth flight

Secret wings unfold out of side

Agent Shiftwell

High-tech Holley has big expectations of her spy equipment. She has never used them in the field before and cannot wait to test them on her first secret mission. Holley insists on being outfitted with only the most cutting-edge contraptions and grooviest gizmos!

Secret gun hidden in hubcap

SECRET AGENT MATER

A CASE OF MISTAKEN identity sees Mater thrust into an exciting secret mission! With his friendly demeanor, big mouth, and rusty exterior, Mater has the perfect disguise—nobody will ever suspect that a tow truck from Radiator Springs would be working closely with British Intelligence. Pretty soon, Mater proves he is just as brave as Finn and Holley!

Espionage Adventure

Agents Finn and Holley think Mater is a top secret agent and is just the tow truck to find out what the Lemons are up to. To be a top secret agent, you need the perfect disguise. However, Mater might stand out a little too much in these disguises!

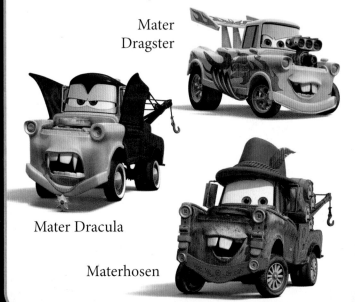

Mater Dragster

Mater Dracula

Materhosen

American agent Rod "Torque" Redline mistakes Mater for a secret agent and plants a hidden device on him. The device contains a very important photograph.

Parachute for daring airborne rescues

Mater will never change his rusty appearance!

Disguises and Surprises

Rocket-powered jets and computer-generated disguises are just some of the hidden extras that allow Agent Mater to complete his mission. However, he refuses to get rid of the dents that remind him of his friendship with Lightning.

FRIENDS FALLOUT

ONE IS A HOT-SHOT race car and the other is a rusty tow truck, but that doesn't stop Lightning and Mater from being the best of pals. However, life at the World Grand Prix tests the pair's friendship to its limits. A disastrous race in Tokyo looks like the end of the road for Lightning and Mater. Can they ever get their friendship back on track?

Lightning is focused on winning the WGP, but luckily Mater is around to help him have some fun!

Out of Trouble

Sometimes Mater does not think before he does things and causes a scene. At the Tokyo WGP party, Lightning wants to make a good impression in front of the world's racing elite. However, Mater is excited by all the new sights and attracts a lot of attention. Embarrassed by Mater's behavior, Lightning tells him that he should act differently.

Wearing the 95 badge always reminds Mater of his friendship with Lightning

Whoops!

During the Tokyo race, Mater gives Lightning tactical advice via the team radio. Unfortunately Mater hears another voice on his headset and gets distracted. Confused by all the chatter, Lightning makes a wrong move and loses the race. With his confidence dented, Mater decides to return to Radiator Springs.

DID YOU KNOW?

Mater introduced Lightning to his favorite pastime— tractor tipping. Now Lightning loves it too!

Friends Reunited

Without Mater around things are not quite the same and Lightning begins to realize that he must accept Mater for who he is. Luckily for Lightning, Mater has a big heart and will do anything for his pals. When Lightning's life is at risk at the WGP, Mater stops at nothing to save his best pal!

Lightning finds it hard not to smile when Mater's around

MATER'S MEMORIES

WHAT AN ADVENTURE! Mater has been on an amazing journey—from sightseeing in Japan and Italy and top secret agent missions in Paris, to saving Lightning in London and meeting the Queen of England. However, despite his round-the-world adventures, Mater wouldn't live anywhere other than Radiator Springs!

Although Mater didn't understand the rules of sumo wrestling, it looked as fun as tractor tipping!

Mater really loved visiting Japan, although he wasn't keen on the Wasabi. Dadgum, that was hot!

SUSHI MASTA!

When cars are exhausted from city sightseeing, they can doze off in a cube motel!

交通渋滞
アイスクリーム

DINOCO
エネルギードリンク

WGP PORTO CORSA INTERNATIONALE

Mater didn't understand what any car said in Tokyo! Next time he visits, he is going to learn Japanese.

Mater didn't do any sightseeing in Porto Corsa—he was far too busy being a secret agent! Maybe next time...

Unfortunately, the Japanese Lightning McClean vacuum cleaner was too heavy to bring back to Radiator Springs!

Mater got a very personal tour of London landmark Big Bentley—he was held prisoner in it by the Lemons!

Mater enjoyed mixing with the Parisian locals. Tomber, the spare parts dealer, was a very interesting character!

Mater saw some spectacular scenery in Tokyo.

Mater didn't understand why some of the Japanese girls carried umbrellas—it wasn't even raining!

Mater might be well-traveled but Radiator Springs will always be home.

Greetings from RADIATOR SPRINGS
GATEWAY TO THE ORNAMENT VALLEY

WGP PORTO CORSA INTERNATIONALE

Meeting the Queen and getting knighted in London was a gas, but being Sir Tow Mater takes a bit of getting used to!

Unfortunately, Mater didn't get to celebrate Lightning's win at Porto Corsa—he was kidnapped by the Lemons!

JUG JUG

LONDON, NEW YORK, MELBOURNE,
MUNICH, AND DELHI

Editor Jo Casey
Designer Mark Richards
Jacket designed by Toby Truphet
Managing Art Editor Ron Stobbart
Publishing Manager Catherine Saunders
Art Director Lisa Lanzarini
Associate Publisher Simon Beecroft
Category Publisher Alex Allan
Production Editor Siu Yin Chan
Production Controller Nick Seston

First published in the United States in 2011
by DK Publishing
375 Hudson Street, New York, New York 10014

This paperback edition published in the United States in 2011

10 9 8 7 6 5 4 3 2 1
007—178514—May/11

Page design copyright ©2011 Dorling Kindersley Limited

Published in Great Britain by Dorling Kindersley Limited.

DK books are available at special discounts when purchased in bulk for sales
promotions, premiums, fund-raising, or educational use.
For details, contact: DK Publishing Special Markets,
375 Hudson Street, New York, New York 10014.
SpecialSales@dk.com

A catalog record for this book is available from the Library of Congress.

ISBN: 978-0-7566-8884-4

Color reproduction by Media Development Printing Ltd, UK
Printed and bound in China by Toppan

Dorling Kindersley would like to thank:
LeighAnna MacFadden, Kelly Bonbright, Geoff Yetter, Leeann Alameda,
Cherie Hammond, Clay Welch, Desiree Mourad, Holly Lloyd,
Silvia Palara, Jesse Weglein, Angie Mistretta, Magen Farrar, Dawn Rivers,
Tim Zohr, Brian Tanaka, and Britney Best at Pixar Animation Studios.
Laura Uyeda, Scott Tilley, Scott Piehl, Tony Fejeran, Shiho Tilley,
Chelsea Alon, and Lauren Kressel at Disney Publishing.

Discover more at
www.dk.com